65 YEARS OF INNOVATION

Motorsport is unique among global sports. It involves an additional contributing element over and above the athletic contest between drivers – the cars they drive.

Mankind has had a peculiar fascination for its cars since they first hit the road in the late 19th century. It wasn't too long before human nature took over and people started seeing whose was fastest. Organised racing followed, and soon people began producing vehicles just for competition.

The Second World War interrupted serious motorsport, but once life returned to some normality, and priorities allowed it, motorsport was back.

The Formula 1 World Championship was first contested in 1950. 65 years later, the basics of producing a world champion, either in the Drivers' championship or (since 1958) the Constructors' championship, remain the same. Innovation and technical excellence, well-prepared and reliable, will do it.

Over those 65 years, there have been some truly impressive grand prix cars designed and built, and while there have been some equally brilliant drivers at the top of the sport, the truth remains – without the car to match those skills, even the best are going to struggle.

This publication highlights the cars which, in my view, have stood out in Formula 1 over those 65 years, either as outstandingly successful in a particular era, or as game-changing innovators. Or as just plain quirky.

There is little doubt that some of the biggest leaps forward in Formula 1 design came in the first three decades of grand prix racing – and thus two-thirds of the cars in this selection

"Putting together a 'Best-of' compilation... does remind you of the fascination Formula 1 has always held..."

The greatest F1 innovator of them all – Colin Chapman (centre), with Mario Andretti (left) and Ronnie Peterson at the launch of the extraordinary 'ground-effect' Lotus 79. The pair would dominate the 1978 championship, but their day of triumph would turn to tragedy...

come from that era. Those were simpler, heady, 'seat-of-the-pants' days; ideas came from left field, sketched on restaurant napkins – and there were some brilliant ones.

More recently, spiraling costs have seen F1 become more and more tightly regulated (and it is, of course, big business globally – with nearly three times as many races as there once were each year). Under those circumstances, major radical innovation becomes all but impossible – but, nevertheless, it is still innovation and the pushing of boundaries, which stands one car out above the rest.

Double-diffusers; 'off-throttle' blown diffusers; 'Power Units' with ERS... who would have contemplated the hi-tech of 21st century Formula 1, when such major brainstorms as putting the

engine in the back, building cars out of aluminium sheet, or discovering carbon fibre were milestones in earlier times?

Could the Mercedes engineers, who put together the company's world-beating 1954 W196 grand prix car, have possibly imagined the exquisite piece of technological art the company would deliver 60 years later?

Putting together a 'Best-of' compilation such as this does remind you of the fascination Formula 1 has always held – there have been some truly awesome, revolutionary cars in Formula 1, dreamed up by very smart people along the way, and I guess that, regardless of the politics and the money-driven business it has become, it will always be the case.

– *Chris Lambden*

1950-1951
ALFA ROMEO 158/159
FAST OUT OF THE BLOCKS

ALFA ROMEO 158/159

In 1950, motorsport restarted after the Second World War, and one manufacturer was truly ready to go, dominating the first ever F1 Championship (called the F1 European Championship, despite one of its seven rounds being the American Indianapolis 500).

Alfa Romeo's pretty little 158 had been a pre-war success story, competing in what was known as voiturette racing (effectively second-level racing) in 1.5 litre form. In that sense, the car was well-developed at the least.

It was typical of the race car design of the time: front-engined with tubular chassis and hand-crafted aluminium bodywork, fuel tank behind the driver, drum brakes, and very little of what today would be termed "aerodynamics".

The regulations for the first championship in 1950 were announced in 1947, permitting 1500cc supercharged or 4500cc normally-aspirated engines. Alfa thus produced a supercharged version of its existing straight-eight cylinder 1497cc engine. It put out over 300hp.

While new manufacturers such as Ferrari scrambled to design and develop new cars, not even contesting some of the early races, the Alfa Romeo 158 – basically a 1938 design, remember – cleaned up, winning all six European-based Grands Prix (none of the teams ventured to the US for Indy).

Even so, unreliability played its part in deciding the final outcome of the championship. Works drivers Giuseppe Farina (above and below) and Juan-Manuel Fangio had three wins each, but the latter had three DNFs to Farina's one and, with drivers counting their best four results, the championship went to the Italian.

"Alfa Romeo's pretty little 158 had been a pre-war success story..."

"In 1950, the only time an Alfa didn't lead a race was during refueling."

Alfa Romeo dominated the constructors' points though.

The car was updated for 1951 – the 159 featured a (non-independent) De Dion rear axle (replacing the previous 'swing' axle), and horsepower was up to over 400. But time and more modern designs were catching up with Alfa. Bigger and bigger superchargers had provided power gain, but at the cost of massive fuel consumption. In 1950, the only time an Alfa didn't lead a race was during refueling, but in 1951 the problem escalated. The engine was now, compared to the new breed – especially Ferrari's all-new 4.5-litre unsupercharged engines – outdated.

Nevertheless, while the Ferraris found their feet and suffered a few developmental DNFs, Fangio still managed to win four races (out of seven) and take the 1951 title.

Facing the cost of all-new design and development to keep up, and unable to convince the Italian government to chip in (why would they – Ferrari was on the up?), Alfa quit F1 at the end of the year.

"Bigger and bigger superchargers had provided power gain, but at the cost of massive fuel consumption."

1954-1955
MERCEDES W196
ENTER THE GERMANS

MERCEDES W196

With 1952 and 1953 being 'interim' Formula 2-based world championship years as teams struggled with the cost of F1 re-entry, 1954 provided the first real opportunity for new F1 teams. Enter Mercedes, complete with some of the technology developed during the war on German fighter planes.

Faced with the choice between a 2.5 litre normally-aspirated engine or a relatively tiny 750cc supercharged option, Mercedes did its research and concluded that, for the first time in over 30 years, it would be best-served with the 2.5 litre option.

They produced a quad-cam fuel-injected 'straight-eight' engine (effectively two four-cylinder blocks joined end-on-end), with all-new 'desmodronic' valves with a five-speed (as opposed to rivals' four) gearbox. Initially producing around 260bhp, 12 months' development raised the engine's output to 290hp.

The W196 chassis was a space-frame design using small-diameter tubes, with inboard brakes (they

Modern era Mercedes stars Michael Schumacher and Nico Rosberg demonstrated both the openwheeler and 'streamliner' versions of the W196 at the Nürburgring in 2011.

> *"What set it apart, thanks to a loophole in the regulations, was Mercedes' decision to create an all-enveloping, 'streamliner' body."*

wouldn't fit inside the wheels!). Suspension was by dual wishbones and torsion bars at the front and swing axles with torsion bars at the rear.

What set it apart, thanks to a loophole in the regulations, was Mercedes' decision to create an all-enveloping, 'streamliner' body for the car, which worked very well on high-speed circuits with limited cornering requirements. However, drivers Fangio, Karl Kling and Hans Hermann found it difficult to 'place' the car in this spec on tighter race circuits, and an 'openwheeler' version was also created. There were also three wheelbase options available. Mercedes was nothing if not thorough.

The team first appeared four races into the nine-race 1954 championship, at the French Grand Prix, with Fangio winning four of the remaining six races. Allied with two wins he'd had prior to the Mercedes debut, with Maserati, he was an easy championship winner.

Rising British star Stirling Moss joined the team in 1955, when the championship consisted of just six European races (plus the Indianapolis 500), shortened following the Le Mans 24 hours sportscar tragedy. Fangio's W196 won four of them along with a second (to Moss in a sister car at the British GP – there were suggestions he followed his team-mate around all day and allowed the win...).

Mercedes' return to grand prix racing was relatively short – the team won nine of the 12 races it contested in 1954 and '55, then withdrew following the Le Mans tragedy, satisfied that it had exhibited a level of superiority in grand prix racing.

One of the 1954 W196 cars, driven by Fangio, was sold in 2013 for a stunning US$29.6m, a world record for a car sold at auction at the time.

1956-1957

MASERATI 250F

ONE FOR THE LITTLE GUYS

MASERATI 250F

While not as out-and-out successful as the Mercedes with which it competed in 1954 and 55, Maserati earned its place in Formula 1 history as the first real 'customer car' supplier to enjoy any real success.

The company took a step forward in 1956 with its revised 'ladder chassis' 250F. A five speed gearbox had already replaced the original transverse four-speed, along with Dunlop disc brakes, but now the 'factory' race cars would benefit from the straight-six engine being tilted by six-degrees to assist aerodynamics and lower the centre of gravity.

With Stirling Moss driving in 1956, Maserati almost took its first championship – this time bowing to Ferrari (and again to Fangio). However, at the end of the year, Fangio returned

Maserati provided the car for the maestro Juan Manuel Fangio's fifth and last world championship.

> ### *"The company was in serious debt, and only continued to exist thanks to support from the Italian government."*

to Maserati (he had won two races for the team in early 1954 before having to honour an agreement to drive the Mercedes W196 when it was ready) – prompting Moss to leave for the British Vanwall team.

Maserati went all-out that year, with a stiffer chassis, and replacing the lightweight six-cylinder engine with a powerful V12 engine which, although ultimately no real gain over the earlier engine, allowed the great man to drive to his fifth world title, and Maserati's one and only (although it had contributed in part to Fangio's 1954 crown).

Fangio won four of the first five races (not including Indianapolis), and while Moss (now in a Vanwall) came on strong to win three, including the last two, the championship was effectively well over by then.

That was the end of Maserati's official involvement in Formula 1 this time around. The company was in serious debt, and only continued to exist thanks to support from the Italian government, which saw no need to go racing – Italy had Ferrari of course. The 250F would appear in private hands for a further season or so before the rear-engined revolution killed it off. Maserati did return to F1, supplying V12 engines to Cooper at the start of the 3-litre formula in 1966, which won two grands prix.

The 250F, though, remains as a classic of its era. Thanks to the numbers of cars produced, especially for 'gentleman' privateers, Maserati 250Fs are a force of numbers in historic racing these days.

> ### *"...Maserati 250Fs are a force of numbers in historic racing..."*

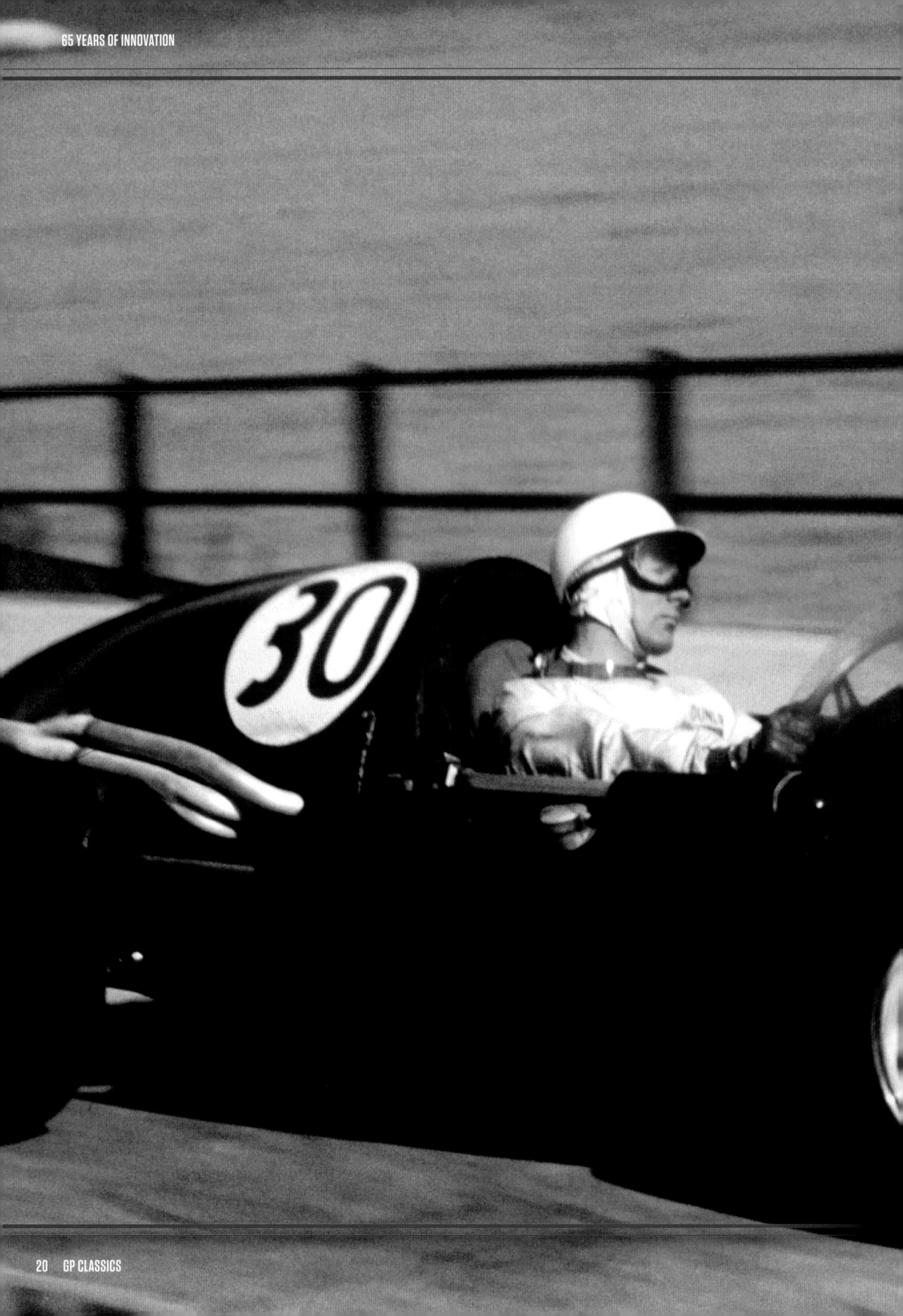
30

1959-1960
COOPER T51
REAR-ENGINED REVOLUTION – SORT OF

COOPER T51

When Jack Brabham drove to sixth place in the 1957 Monaco Grand Prix with a rear-engine Formula 2 Cooper, the die was cast. Stirling Moss then drove the same car (owned by his patron, Rob Walker) to victory in the 1958 Argentine Grand Prix. The revolution was under way.

Rear-engined cars, particularly Coopers, weren't actually new. Who could forget the glorious rear-engine Auto Unions of pre-World War 2 motorsport? And for years, Cooper Cars had been producing 500cc Formula 3 car

powered by a JAP motorcycle engine. Simple expediency prompted them to put the engine in the back, with a chain-drive to the rear axle. Over 300 of the rear-engine cars were sold in the early 50s, but still real racing cars, even Cooper's own F2 cars when it entered the fray, had the engine in the front.

The first step towards motorsport history came with the transformation of Cooper's F3 design into a sports car, powered by a 1098cc four-cylinder Coventry Climax engine. Penned by ex-Vanwall F1 designer

"The T51 was no doubt Cooper's finest hour..."

Owen 'Whiskers' Maddock, the car was among the first to utilise curved tube design (as opposed to straight 'birdcage' style), and it worked well. It was the Cooper 'Bobtail'.

It was Jack Brabham who suggested the team could ultimately develop an F1 version of this chassis and so, initially, Maddock designed a Formula 2 version, which became the car that Brabham and Moss achieved the early eye-catching results.

With a full-on 2.5 litre four-cylinder Coventry Climax engine in the wind (requested by both Coopers and Colin Chapman at fledgling Lotus), Maddock, with Brabham's aggressive input, drew up what was to become the Cooper T51, which would provide the first F1 world championship for a rear-engine car.

Why was the rear-engine Cooper immediately successful? Compared to the front-engine cars it was small, with much-reduced frontal area. With no driveshaft between his legs, the driver could sit lower and the whole centre-of-gravity of the car was lower. It greatly improved weight distribution, and traction to the rear wheels.

The Cooper factory, with drivers Brabham and Bruce McLaren, and Rob Walker's private team (Stirling Moss) ran T51 Coopers in 1959, up against the proven might, and reliability, of Ferrari. The Cooper's weakness was its gearbox, but nevertheless the car won five of the eight grands prix (Brabham 2, Moss 2, McLaren 1) and Brabham legendarily became world champion by pushing his out-of-fuel car over the line at the final race, the US Grand Prix.

For 1960, last year of the 2.5 litre formula, rear-engine cars appeared from Lotus, BRM and Porsche, but the Cooper T51, and latterly the T53, was still the car to beat. Although McLaren took a win and second place in the two openers, 'Black Jack' pounced with five straight wins to take his second title. Coopers thus won every race, other than Monaco and the US Grand Prix, won by Moss, now in a rear-engine Lotus 18.

From the following year, the first of the new 1.5 litre formula, every grand prix car ever built has had the engine in the rear. The T51 was no doubt Cooper's finest hour and, although Cooper's presence in Formula 1 would only last a few more years, the company can lay claim to the most significant development in Formula 1 history.

ack Brabham gave Cooper its first world title in 1959, then backed up in 1960.

Wolfgang Von Tripps, here pictured at Monaco, looked headed for the 1961 Drivers' Championship, but was killed at Monza after his car speared into the crowd.

1961
FERRARI 156F1
BEWARE THE SHARK

FERRARI 156F1

The 1961 F1 season belonged to Ferrari. Dominated by Cooper and the other rear-engine cars in 1960, the Scuderia was well-prepared for the new 1.5 litre Formula 1 (which was pretty much based on the pre-1961 Formula 2 – in which Ferrari had actually debuted the rear-engine 156), while the majority of its opposition were still thinking about it.

With a proven '65-degree' V6 Dino engine – replaced mid-season with an even better '120-degree' V6 – Ferrari had the power jump on its rivals, all starting out with an existing Coventry Climax four-cylinder (some 14kg

"The engine was the ace in the Ferrari 156's armoury."

"The tale of the Ferrari 156 ends in mystery. Not one example of the Ferrari 156s built and raced in that 1961 season remains."

heavier than the Ferrari V6) engine pending the arrival of what would be a superb 1.5 litre V8.

The engine was the ace in the Ferrari 156's armoury. The chassis itself was a reasonably conservative spaceframe design, by the renowned Carlo Chiti, and was Ferrari's first rear-engine F1 car, but had its one distinguishing feature – the 'sharknose'.

Ferrari dominated – the only barrier to a clean sweep coming from the brilliant Stirling Moss, who used all his legendary skill to win on the two 'drivers' circuits – Monaco and the Nürburgring. Otherwise, it was one-way traffic.

The championship would ultimately be decided at the penultimate round. American Phil Hill had proved the qualifying star, with five poles, but German Wolfgang von Tripps the race master, and points leader going to Monza.

It ended tragically, with Von Tripps colliding with rising star Jim Clark on lap two, going into Tamburello. His car speared off into the crowd, killing the driver and 15 spectators. The race, as it did in those days, continued and, unaware of the crash consequences, Hill won the race. That put him a point up on his Ferrari team-mate, the only driver in a position to challenge, and so Hill, on that day, became the first American F1 champion. Ferrari withdrew from the US Grand Prix.

Such was Ferrari's 1961 dominance that his team-mate, American Phil Hill, was the only real challenger to Von Tripps, and by winning that tragic Italian race, Hill became world champion.

The F156 remained in service for two more seasons, albeit with a more conventional nose, but in technical terms British teams, and their rapid technical development of both cars and engines, soon overtook it. In 1964, pretty much as a back-up car, the F156 won its last race, the Austrian Grand Prix, driven by Lorenzo Bandini, on a horrendously bumpy Zeltweg track, where all the opposition's cars fell out with suspension-related failures.

The tale of the Ferrari 156 ends in mystery. Not one example of the Ferrari 156s built and raced in that 1961 season remains. Enzo Ferrari, it is said, had them all cut up and destroyed. No-one knows for sure why, but it is speculated that the tragic events at Monza may have had something to do with the Commendatore's state of mind. Another suggestion is that Enzo was furious at the departure of several key staff – including chief engineer Chiti and sporting director Tavoni – after a major dispute just weeks after the end of that season.

Either way, sadly, no genuine relic of a tumultuous, but successful, year in Ferrari's history remains.

> "…no genuine relic of a tumultuous, but successful, year in Ferrari's history remains."

Ferrari still raced the F156 in 1962, but the rest had by then caught up and Hill (#1), after managing a second and two thirds in the first three races of the season, didn't mount the podium again and finished a distant sixth in the championship.

1962-1965

LOTUS 25

CHAPMAN'S FIRST REVOLUTION

Archetypical Clark/Lotus 25 image, from the 1964 British Grand Prix. Clark won, but reliability issues cost him, and Lotus, the championship that year.

LOTUS 25

"1963, though, was a landmark year: 10 races, seven wins. It was all over after the Italian Grand Prix in September."

While breakthrough individual designs and concepts have peppered Formula 1's history, the creator of the most radical, innovative, and championship-winning cars was undoubtedly Colin Chapman – and the first of these was the exquisite Lotus 25.

While 'stressed-skin' construction was certainly not new – the aeronautical world had been going down this path for many years – the concept of building a racing car without its traditional tubular frame was one of the biggest technical steps ever in Formula 1.

Folklore has it, and in this case it's correct, that the initial sketches for the design that would revolutionise Formula 1, were on a table napkin, as Chapman outlined his thoughts to Frank Costin, the former Vanwall F1 car designer who now worked at Lotus on bodywork design.

The concept was amazingly simple – a pair of strong rear (immediately behind the driver) and front (just beyond the driver's feet) bulkheads were joined by long, aluminium box sections, with a third less structural bulkhead across the drivers legs, locating the dash. Structurally, this was much stiffer and lighter, than the existing tubular-framed cars. The box sections continued back beyond the rear bulkhead, allowing for mounting of the engine and rear suspension – something Chapman would eliminate in his next radical car, six years later …

"…the initial sketches for the design that would revolutionise Formula 1, were on a table napkin…"

In the meantime, there were other advantages of the 'monocoque' construction. The long side box sections also now contained the fuel tanks (previously behind the driver). This allowed the driver to lay back, so that his chin was almost on his chest – unheard of – and so there was a significant reduction in frontal area as well. The chassis became known, understandably, as 'the bathtub'.

The design and development of the Lotus 25 coincided with the release of British engine manufacturer Coventry Climax's answer to the Ferrari V6 engine, which had dominated the opening year (1961) of the 1.5 litre formula – the 1498cc Coventry Climax V8.

The Lotus 25 thus had the engine performance to match its chassis and with the added brilliance of Jim Clark at the wheel, went on a victorious charge, broken

only by the occasional reliability issue. In 1962, Clark's main rival was Graham Hill in the ultra-reliable BRM – indeed in a nine-race season, Hill would have won easily were it not for the 'best six results only to count' system, which saw three Clark retirements nullified. Clark led the final, deciding race, only for the engine to develop an oil leak, Handing the race, and title to Hill.

1963, though, was a landmark year: 10 races, seven wins. It was all over after the Italian Grand Prix in September – five wins from seven races.

1964 looked like more of the same – three wins in the first five races, but then a string of engine issues allowed Hill and John Surtees (Ferrari) to catch up. Again it was a last race decider and again Clark had it in the bag until a penultimate lap engine failure handed the title to Surtees.

"The Lotus 25 was a landmark in Formula 1"

The following year was probably Clark's (and Lotus') best. The Lotus 33 – an updated Lotus 25, stiffer and stronger – was introduced, with Clark switching between both. After seven races, Clark had won six – he literally missed the seventh in Monaco, as he was away in America, taking a historic Indianapolis 500 win, for Lotus of course... The third of those 1965 wins, the French Grand Prix, was Clark's last start in a Lotus 25 and the 25's last F1 win.

The Lotus 25 was a landmark in Formula 1. Its aluminium monocoque construction set the agenda for Formula 1 car construction for nearly two decades – only superseded with the arrival of aeronautical composites in Grand Prix racing. On that alone, and like the earlier Cooper T51, it too could be considered the most significant F1 car of all time. The choice is yours.

THE DEBATE:
Did Clark make Lotus or did Lotus make Clark?

There is no doubt that Jim Clark and Colin Chapman constituted a Superteam – Clark's speed and finesse allied with Chapman's ingenuity and design innovation. Together they were all but unbeatable.

But, as some Formula 1 historians ask, was Clark the defining ingredient? Certainly, throughout this era, Clark mostly had team-mates who were no match. In fact, a second Lotus 25 only scored two third-place podiums throughout the car's life – Brit Peter Arundell taking both at the start of 1964 before a serious Formula 2 crash put him out of racing for over a year.

Our verdict? The Lotus 25 was a revolutionary trend-setter, which delivered significant performance gains – let's face it, the race was on among the opposition to create their own aluminium monocoque chassis from the day they first saw Chapman's creation.

But there's little doubt that Clark too was one level above the rest – his brand of precision, feel and mechanical sympathy is what got the Lotus 25 to the finish line, up front, when the sister car often didn't. Chapman's achilles heel was reliability – particularly structural – as he aimed for the lightest car possible, and Clark's sympathetic style was thus an imperative.

As a duo, the pair created Grand Prix history.

1966-1967

BRABHAM-REPCO BT19/20

AUSSIE INGENUITY

BRABHAM-REPCO BT19/20

When it was announced in 1963 that Formula 1 would double its engine capacity from 1.5 litres to 3 litres from the start of 1966, few would guess how unprepared most of the major teams would be.

Coventry Climax, who had supplied engines to so many teams during the 1.5-litre era pulled out, Ferrari committed to trying its heavy V12 sports car engine, and others were... well... floundering.

Not so for Australian Jack Brabham – although he too had some issues to sort as 1966 approached. The successful company he founded with compatriot Ron Tauranac, Motor Racing Developments, was flat-out producing 'production' F2, F3, and other cars, including the F1 cars used by Jack Brabham Racing, which ran the Grand Prix race programme separately. Tauranac was unhappy with his reduced, 'arms' length' F1 involvement and almost gave it away... fortunately they agreed to merge the businesses, and life, and a successful chapter, went on.

The story of the 1966-67 BT19 Repco Brabham is equally as much about its engine as it is the car.

It is something of an incorrect legend that Australian company Repco created its Oldsmobile-based V8 for Jack's F1 effort. In fact the engine already existed, in the planning stages at least, as a 2.5-litre 'Tasman Series' engine for the antipodean F1-style series run in Australia

While Brabham won his 1966 championship with the well-used test 'mule', the single BT19 ever built, team-mate Denny Hulme (this page and opposite) was first to get his hands on the first built-for-purpose car, the BT20.

"...those unique stats hide the sheer audacity and inventiveness responsible for that 1966 championship victory – in a car never initially designed for the job, with an engine put together half way around the world."

and New Zealand every January and February in those days. It was, of course, only a small step to convince Repco that a 3-litre version might well do the business in F1 as well.

But consider the logistics – a Formula 1 team manufacturing and racing cars out of the UK and an engine being developed and produced on the opposite side of the world. And this is 1965, remember – no electronic communications, no faxes; just phones and post. Colour television hadn't yet been introduced in either the UK or Australia...

The first engine was mated to a one-off Brabham car, the BT19, originally designed in 1965 to take the last of the Climax 1.5-litre engines. Jack and Ron considered, with the Repco engine's modest weight (160kg), that the BT19 could handle the 310bhp, initially at least.

The car debuted bizarrely at a January 1, 1966, South African Grand Prix, made up of a hotch-potch of now-superseded 1.5-litre cars... and Jack's BT19, the only new 3-litre car present. Pole, the race lead and fastest lap came quite easily, but the car retired with a fuel pump problem.

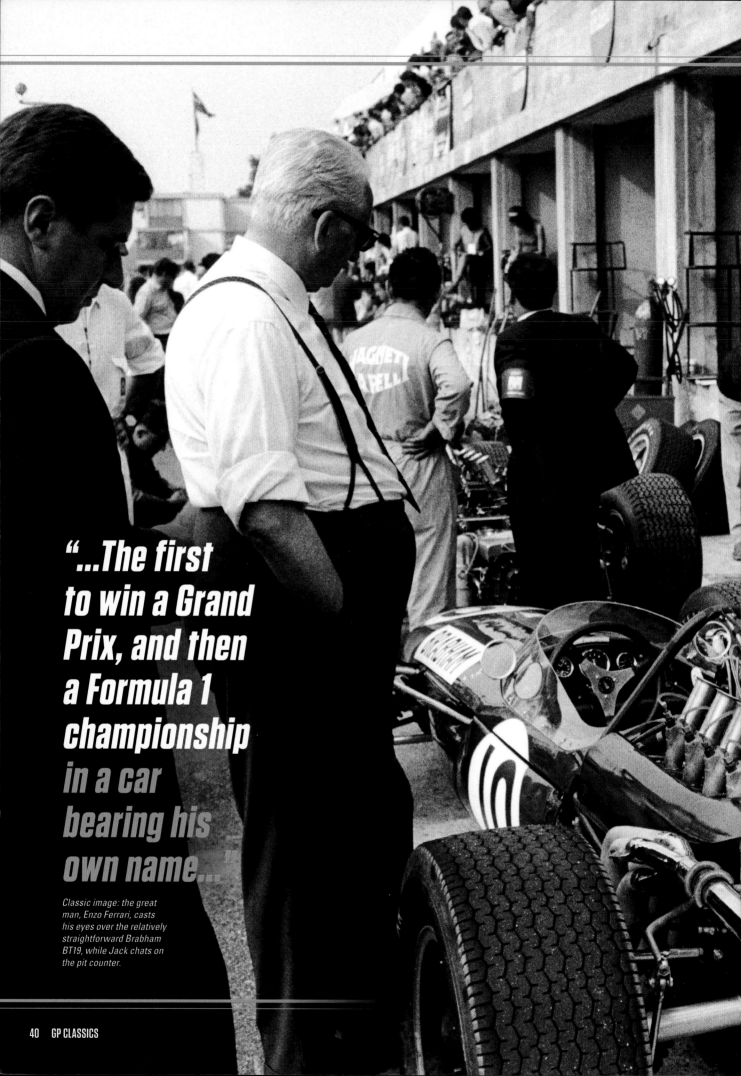

"...The first to win a Grand Prix, and then a Formula 1 championship in a car bearing his own name..."

Classic image: the great man, Enzo Ferrari, casts his eyes over the relatively straightforward Brabham BT19, while Jack chats on the pit counter.

Australians were next to see the fledgling F1 challenger, the BT19 contesting the final two 'Tasman' races of February 1966 in 2.5-litre form. They call it developing on the run! Jack finished the second of these (at Longford in Tasmania) third, behind the championship-dominating 1.9-litre BRMs of Jackie Stewart and Graham Hill. Promising.

And so, Jack embarked on the 1966 season with 'The Old Nail' BT19, albeit with 3-litre Repco V8, while team-mate Denny Hulme had to use a 2.5-litre Climax-powered 'Tasman' car for the two opening races. Neither was spectacular – two DNFs for Jack, a single fourth for Denny.

"Jack embarked on the 1966 season with 'The Old Nail' BT19..."

But then, wham! Jack won four in a row, still in the BT19, while Hulme now had the first purpose-built BT20. Jack retired early in the next race, the Italian Grand Prix, but so vast was his points lead at that stage that the championship was won, with two races to go.

The first to win a Grand Prix, and then a Formula 1 championship in a car bearing his own name: those unique stats hide the sheer audacity and inventiveness responsible for that 1966 championship victory – in a car never initially designed for the job, with an engine put together half way around the world. Amazing!

While Jack had a BT20 for 1967, BT19 still ran in three races, grabbing second in France. These days, the car remains in Repco ownership, in Australia.

41

1967-1970

LOTUS 49

THE PERFECT PACKAGE

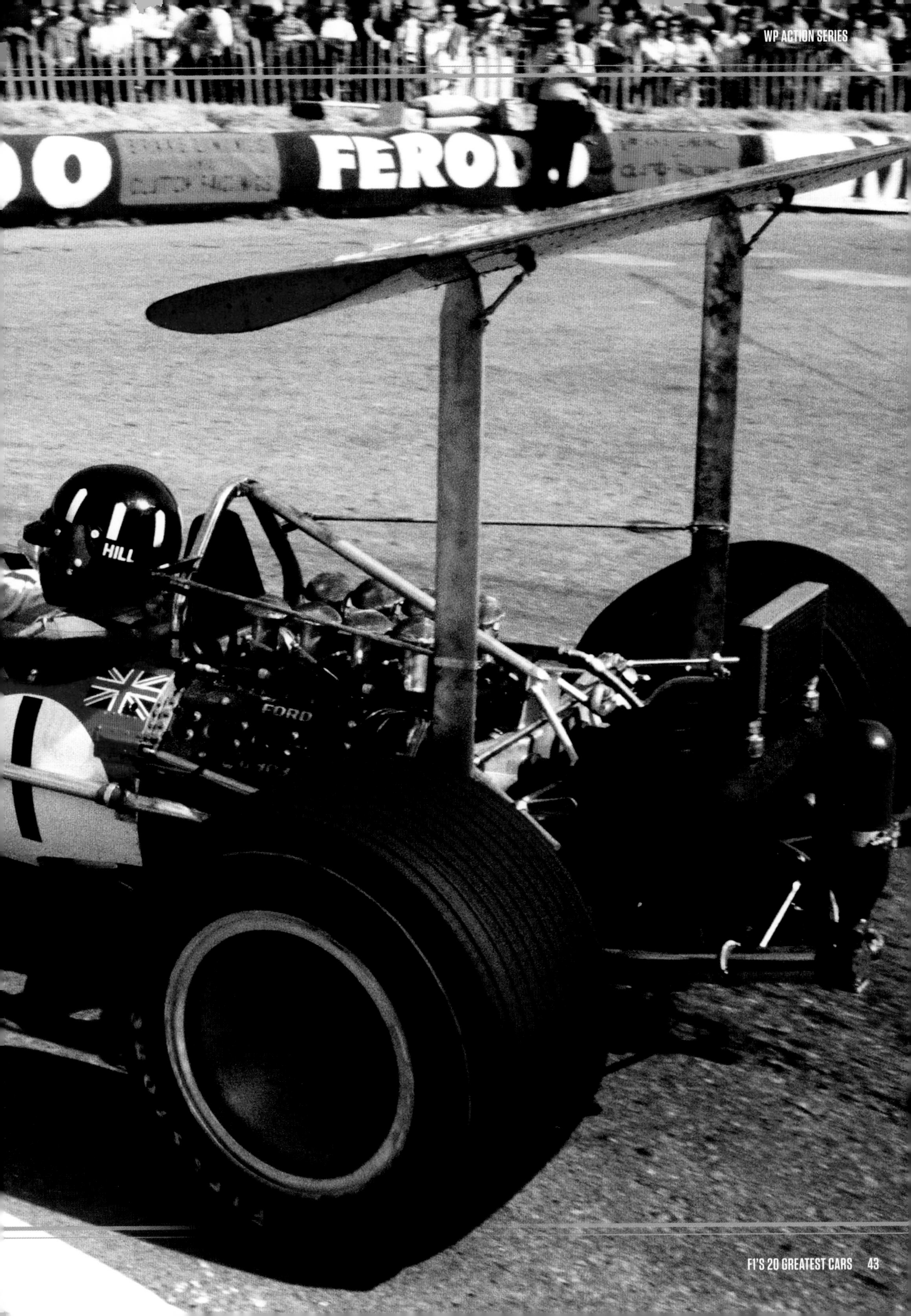
FEROD
HILL
FORD

LOTUS 49

The ungainly H-16 BRM-powered Lotus 43 (top) actually pioneered the concept of the engine as a stressed member of the chassis. The Lotus 49, with its purpose-built Cosworth V8 engine (above) refined it perfectly.

"On April 7, Clark died in a crash during a Formula 2 race at Hockenheim, leaving the team, and the sport reeling."

Colin Chapman's second entry in F1's 20 Greatest Cars is another subject with a degree of urban myth – relating to its construction.

When Formula 1 switched to three-litre engines in 1966, Lotus wasn't ready. There was a plan going on in the background which wouldn't produce anything until 1967, so for 1966 Chapman had agreed terms with BRM to use the company's impressive ('on paper') H-16 engine in the back of what was an evolution of Lotus' successful Indycar, the 38, with which Jim Clark had won the 1965 Indianapolis 500.

The H-16 did however allow for Chapman (and co-designer Maurice Phillipe) to debut their newest concept – the complete lack of chassis structure behind the driver's bulkhead, with the engine attached directly to that bulkhead and the rear suspension mounted off the gearbox and rear or the engine, which thus became a fully stressed structural chassis member.

It was thus actually the 1966 Lotus 43 which pioneered this design revolution, and not the famous car which followed the following year.

While the opposition waited for the Lotus 43 to fold in half in the middle (it didn't – the design subsequently became the standard for all open-wheeler race cars), that was the least of Chapman's problems. The BRM engine was... heavy, down on power and unreliable. A dud. The team struggled through 1966 (somehow Clark jagged a win at the US Grand Prix), and started 1967 with a couple of 2-litre ex-Tasman Series cars until Chapman could finally unveil the engine that was to revolutionise Formula 1 for the next decade. It was the Cosworth DFV, an all-new V8 engine designed by Cosworth for, and funded by, Ford (see breakout), powering Chapman's evolution of the 43, the exquisite Lotus 49.

Chapman had exclusive use of the engine for 1967 only but, apart from a few teething troubles and an initially 'light-switch'-styled power delivery, the Lotus 49-Cosworth was a winner, tailor-made to utilize the

new Ford. The '67 championship, however, went to Brabham-mounted Denny Hulme, though a pair of strong wins at the end of the season, along with a former champion, Graham Hill, alongside Clark for the first time, boded well for 1968.

Clark won the opening 1968 race, In South Africa, as well as the Australasian Tasman Series in a 2.5-litre version, but then tragedy struck. On April 7, Clark died in a crash during a Formula 2 race at Hockenheim, leaving the

"...When Formula 1 switched to three-litre engines in 1966, Lotus wasn't ready."

team, and the sport reeling. As Ferrari driver Chris Amon articulated, "If it could happen to him, what chance do the rest of us have?"

It was left to Hill to pull the team together, and he did so, winning the next two races before a string of technical failures almost cost him the championship as the now Ford-powered cars of Jackie Stewart (Matra) and Hulme (McLaren) closed in. But a tense final race provided victory, and the title, to Hill.

1969 saw the arrival of aerodynamics as a new and somewhat risky addition to the performance equation. The Lotus 49 that year was typified by the huge wings mounted on struts, high above the car – until after several structural failures, for Hill and new recruit Jochen Rindt, the FIA insisted that wings be mounted to the bodywork of the car.

With Ken Tyrrell's Matra team now refining its Ford-powered car in the hands of the stellar Jackie Stewart, JYS dominated and easily won his first title, although Hill

"...the Lotus 49 nevertheless remains one of the landmark cars..."

took victory at Monaco and Rindt at the US Grand Prix late in the season. This was the race in which Hill crashed heavily, rolling his car and was thrown out, breaking his legs badly. It paved the way for Rindt to lead Team Lotus to success – albeit tragic success – in 1970, mostly in Chapman's next success story, the Lotus 72.

The 49 remained in use early in that season, winning its last race, Monaco, in Rindt's hands. In all, over three years, the Lotus 49 won 12 out of 35 grands prix contested – and it could so easily have been more. Chapman's obsession with lightweight components led to some of the car's race-costing failures, and almost a split with Rindt, who became seriously, and poignantly, concerned over the failure rate.

While there have been more dominant cars in F1's history, the Lotus 49 nevertheless remains one of the landmark cars and a contributor to Chapman's design visionary tag.

Austrian Jochen Rindt, Lotus Cosworth 49B, was leading the 1969 Spanish Grand Prix (run through Barcelona's Montjuich Park) by a huge margin when he suffered a rear wing failure at over 160mph (255km/h). His crash, and a later one in the same race for team-mate Graham Hill was caused by structural failure of the rear wing mounting uprights, designed to get the wing as high, and up into clear air, as possible. High-mount wings were banned shortly thereafter.

FORD COSWORTH DFV
The engine which dominated for a decade

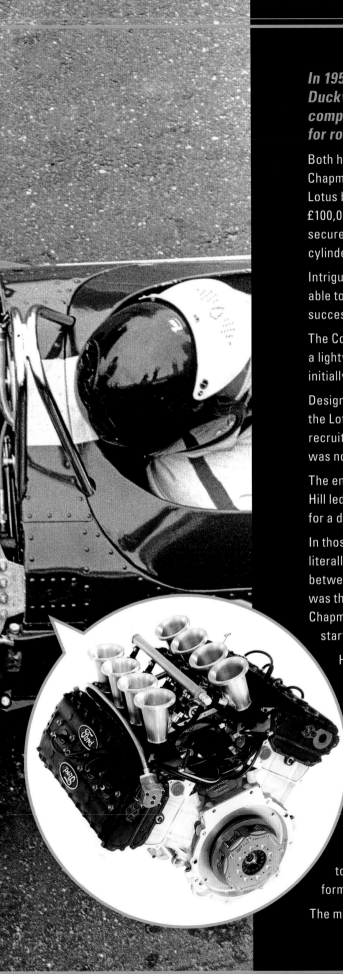

In 1958 a Pair of Englishmen, Mike Costin and Keith Duckworth (Cos and worth) founded a small engineering company, Cosworth, initially providing 'go-faster' parts for road-going Ford car engines, such as the Anglia.

Both had previously worked for and remained on great terms with Chapman and, with the new 3-litre F1 approaching, suggested to the Lotus boss that they could build a competitive engine if a budget of £100,000 (or somewhere between £3-4m in today's terms) could be secured. (In fact, the project consisted of firstly, a 1.5-litre four-cylinder engine, then effectively 'doubled' to create the 3-litre V8).

Intriguingly, while Ford itself was cool on the project, Chapman was able to sell the idea to Ford's UK PR chief, Walter Hayes, who in turn successfully sold the idea to Detroit.

The Cosworth DFV (Double Four Valve) was thus conceived – a lightweight (140kg), 90-degree V8, with four valves-per-cylinder, initially producing 408bhp and 370Nm of torque.

Design and construction of the engine proceeded alongside that of the Lotus 49, with much of the initial testing handled by Lotus new recruit, former world champion Graham Hill, as superstar Jim Clark was now living in France thanks to some tax issues.

The engine, and car, debuted at the 1967 Dutch Grand Prix. Hill led from pole but retired, leaving Clark to nurse his car home for a debut win.

In those early days, budgets remained tight, the team having to literally contest early races without a spare engine, rebuilding between races. By season's end, though, it was obvious that this was the engine for success in F1 and, with Ford not guaranteeing Chapman exclusivity beyond 1967, the queue to buy the engine started to grow.

Hill's F1 Drivers Championship win in 1968 heralded an unbelievable run of success for the Ford Cosworth DFV: 155 championship grand prix wins, 12 Drivers championships in 15 years to 1982 (only broken by three Ferrari wins in 1975, 1977 and 1979) and 10 Constructors titles over the same period, shared between Lotus, Matra, Tyrrell, McLaren and Williams. Some years, the only cars in a large F1 field not powered by the DFV were Ferraris, such was the Cosworth's availability to all, and its reasonable cost.

In the end, the advancing turbo technology slowly signaled the end of Cosworth DFV dominance, but the engine went on to a significant second career, in modified 2.6-litre turbocharged form, powering US CART/Champcars.

The most significant engine in F1 history? Without doubt.

LOTUS 72

AERODYNAMICS SETS THE AGENDA

LOTUS 72

"Back-to-back testing showed the 72, with the same engine/gearbox as a 49, to be nearly 20km/h faster in a straight line."

The car that took over from the Lotus 49, in 1970, took a great car and made it even better. The new world of aerodynamics was now key, especially as most of the serious opposition, Ferrari aside, was now powered by the same ubiquitous Ford DFV V8 engine.

Again designed by Maurice Phillipe, under Chapman's direction, the 72 for the first time moved the radiator from the front of the car to twin sidepods, allowing for the classic 'wedge' shape of the Lotus 72's front. Front and rear wings had grown and, in order to maintain ride height as evenly as possible (an aerodynamic aid), new 'anti-squat' (front) and 'anti-dive' (rear) suspension geometry was tested.

A reduction in 'unsprung weight' was also achieved by moving the brakes 'inboard', the fronts connected to the wheels by hollow driveshafts. This was to prove a tragic innovation.

The changes were, generally, a great success, although the anti-dive and anti-squat suspensions provided a weird feel for the drivers and were removed in an early revamp.

What remained was another Chapman worldbeater. Back-to-back testing showed the 72, with the same engine/gearbox as a 49, to be nearly 20km/h faster in a straight line – an advantage that took team leader, the spectacular Austrian Jochen Rindt, to four consecutive wins in mid-season and a significant championship points lead.

"...the car that took over from the Lotus 49, in 1970, took a great car and made it even better."

Inboard front brakes were a feature of the Lotus 72, but it was the failure of one of these which precipitated Jochen Rindt's fatal crash at Monza.

However, the Italian Grand Prix, at the high-speed Monza circuit, was to prove disastrous. While testing the car in practice, without its wings for even greater straightline speed, the right-front hollow inboard brake shaft on Rindt's car broke under heavy braking for the fast Parabolica corner. This pitched the car off the track and into badly serviced Armco fencing, which parted, allowing the car to hit a post head-on. The Austrian, fearful of the fiery crashes which had claimed so many, had taken to not using the fifth (crotch) strap on the five-point harness (in order to get out of the car quicker), but in this situation, the driver simply slid under the remaining belts and suffered fatal throat injuries.

While a court found his death was due to the badly installed barriers, it was a mechanical failure which initiated the crash. Rindt himself had written to Chapman outlining his fear of mechanical failure in the built-down-to-the-minimum Lotuses, imploring him to strengthen key elements, but it seems little had been done at this point.

With three races to go after Monza, the only challenger to Rindt's points total was Ferrari's Jacky Ickx. Lotus missed the Canadian race, but returned for the penultimate race, the US GP, with newly promoted young Brazilian Emerson Fittipaldi heading the team. His victory that day meant that Ickx couldn't catch Rindt, who thus became F1's first and only posthumous world champion to date.

Fittipaldi was still only just 24 years old when the 1971 season began and, with the team also experimenting with a turbine-powered car on and off, it was a struggle season, but with a refined version of the car, the 72D, liveried in the now legendary black and gold colours of John Players, Fittipaldi took five wins in 1972 (to Stewart's four), sewing up the title, poignantly at Monza, with two races to go.

Another young star, Swede Ronnie Peterson, joined Lotus in 1973 alongside Fittipaldi. Each won three races... but Jackie Stewart at the peak of his powers won five in his final season, took the championship, and retired from racing.

"*Another young star, Swede Ronnie Peterson, joined Lotus in 1973 alongside Fittipaldi. Each won three races...*"

Lotus 72 at its best – Peterson leads defending champion Fittipaldi – 1973.

1973-1977

McLAREN M23

THE FIRST OF MANY

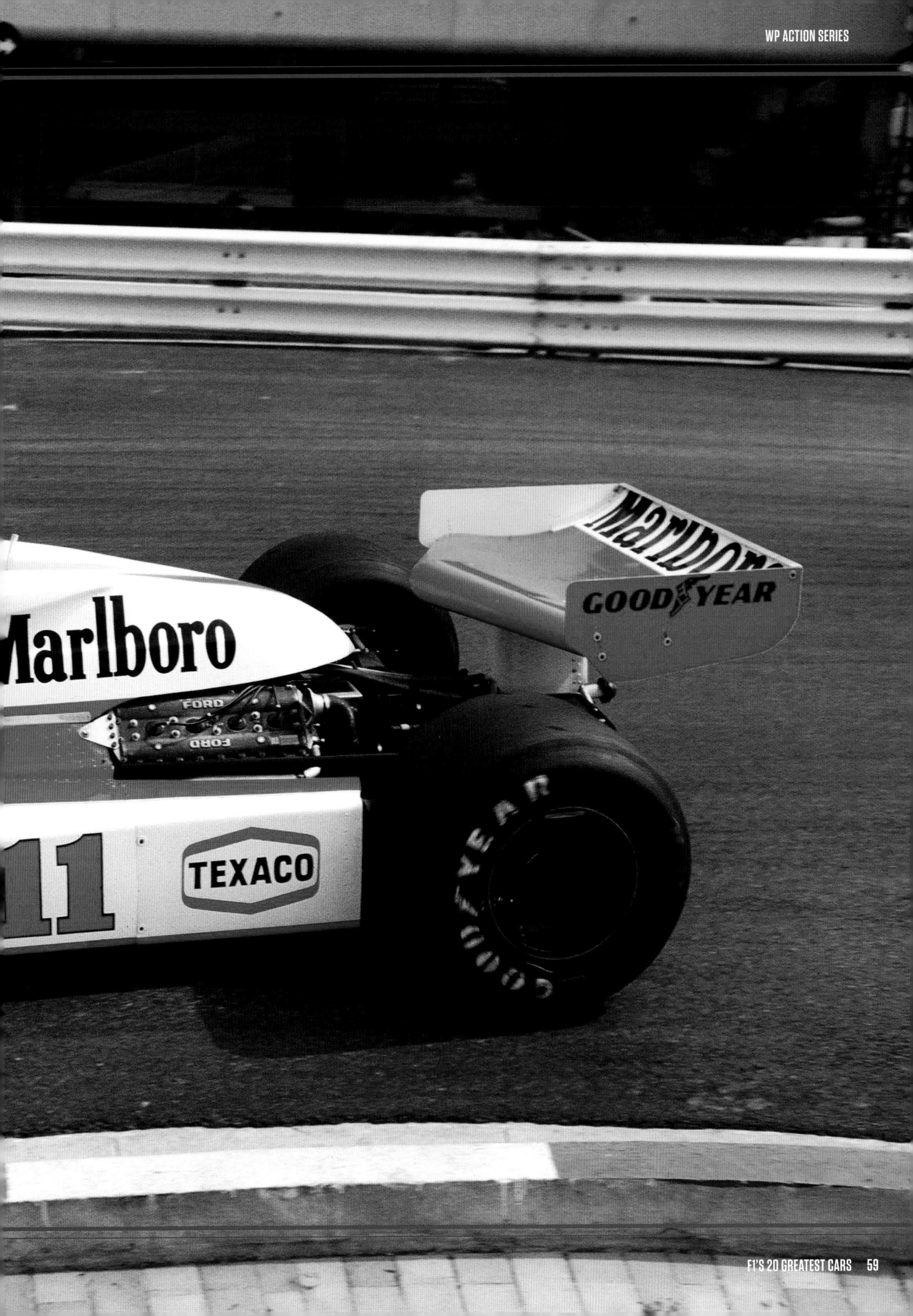
Marlboro
GOODYEAR
FORD
FORD
11
TEXACO
GOODYEAR

McLAREN M23

"Two significant elements arrived at McLaren that year – young Brazilian star Emerson Fittipaldi (who had won the 1972 championship for Lotus)... and Marlboro."

The McLaren M23 might not quite have been the most successful McLaren of all time (check out the MP4/4 elsewhere in this publication), but it was certainly the car which first took the company to the top of the F1 tree and confirmed its presence as a long-term player in grand prix racing.

It could so easily have been otherwise. The death of Bruce McLaren, founder and cornerstone of the team, in a testing crash in 1970 could easily have signaled the end were it not for the sheer determination of his friend and team driver Denny Hulme, with the ongoing management of American Teddy Mayer. At this stage, success in North America largely funded McLaren's F1 programme. They succeeded in Can Am racing and subsequently Indycar – including the Indianapolis 500, which a McLaren, the M16 – designed by up-and-coming designer Gordon Coppuck – won in 1972.

While the Indycar success continued through to the mid-70s, Coppuck had unsurprisingly been drafted to head McLaren's F1 design team, and it was he who conceived the M23, which debuted in 1973.

"The M23 was upgraded for that year, a move from a five - to a six-speed Hewland gearbox..."

The car bore heritage from the successful M16 Indycar, but for the first time incorporated (required by new regulations) a 'deformable' structure. Inboard front suspension allowed clearer airflow through to the rest of the car.

It won three races in that first year, one to Hulme and two to American Peter Revson (*above*), but it was 1974 which was to prove pivotal. Two significant elements arrived at McLaren that year – young Brazilian star Emerson Fittipaldi (who had won the 1972 championship for Lotus) and Marlboro. The latter was to be a long and productive association.

Grand Prix wins were shared by no less than seven drivers in 1974 – it was a close contest. Fittipaldi won three, as did his Lotus replacement Ronnie Peterson, but the Lotus suffered from reliability issues and Peterson only finished fifth in the championship! In the end, a single win, and machine-like consistency would see Clay Regazzoni (Ferrari) and Fittipaldi go the final race of the year level on points, with Jody Scheckter (Tyrrell) an outside chance.

'Emmo' did all he needed to, finishing fourth after Regazzoni's Ferrari struck handling problems, and McLaren had its first world Drivers' championship (along with the Constructors' crown). Hulme had won the opening race, but at season's end announced his retirement.

McLaren bowed to the might of Ferrari and Niki Lauda in 1975, Fittipaldi taking second in the championship, before surprisingly quitting the team to drive for a new team being run by his brother Wilson, Fittipaldi Motorsport. With most top drivers contracted, that left the door open for the flambuoyant James Hunt to join the team for 1976.

The M23 was upgraded for that year, a move from a five - to a six-speed Hewland gearbox the prime change, along with improved aerodynamics and a modest weight-reduction programme.

This was the dramatic season in which Lauda raced to an early championship lead, Hunt started to catch him, Hunt was disqualified after winning in Britain, Lauda crashed in Germany and missed two more races, and it all came down to that dreary wet day in Japan – where

Lauda retired his car in the appalling conditions and Hunt came back from a desperate late tyre puncture to grab third place and the championship – by a single point.

In the end, Hunt won six races in 1976, Lauda five.

During 1977, the M23 was gradually replaced by the new M26 McLaren. Its final outing, though, was to prove significant, the team running a third car, its last M23, at the British Grand Prix to try out a rapid young Canadian by the name of Villeneuve. Gilles qualified ninth and ran as high as fourth before a faulty temperature gauge meant a pit-stop, dropping him out of contention. The point had been made, though, and F1 historians to this day wonder why McLaren team boss Mayer didn't take up the option he had on the future superstar...

Regardless, it was a dramatic and fitting end to the M23's career, which reaped 16 wins, two Drivers' championships and one Constructors' title. It set McLaren on the road.

1975-1980

FERRARI 312T

LAST OF THE 12-CYLINDER SYMPHONIES

FERRARI 312T

"...this was Lauda's 'screw you' moment and, still unhappy at the lack of support from the team following the 1976 crash, he declined to race at the last two races."

The 312T series of Ferraris were the last of the glorious-sounding Flat-12-engined cars, with two banks of six cylinders horizontally opposed, which were able to challenge the hordes of ubiquitous, Ford V8-powered cars which preceded the turbo era of the 80s.

Spearheaded by the great Niki Lauda, who won championships in 1975 and 1977 (and who, but for his

horrendous crash in 1976, would've taken a third), and subsequently 1979 champion Jody Scheckter, Ferrari enjoyed a period of success following the appointment of racing director Luca dì Montezemolo in 1974. He had in turn recalled engineer Mauro Forghieri to the team. That year, the team, with a much-modified version of its previous 312 B3 car, now with shorter wheelbase and side radiators, almost won the championship,

Clay Regazzoni just beaten by Emerson Fittipaldi (McLaren), but it was the 312T, debuting at the start of 1975, which became the defining Ferrari of the era.

The 'T' stood for 'transversale' – a new (sideways mounted) transverse gearbox allowed the car to have a further-shortened wheelbase and better weight distribution. Added to significant rear wing – and unique full front wing – development, and thousands of kilometres of testing by the perfectionist Lauda, Ferrari was back on top. 10 pole positions, five wins and Lauda's first drivers' championship illustrated the sheer technical dominance of the 312T.

It continued into 1976, albeit with a greatly changed 312, the T2. With 'periscope' air intakes banned, ducts now ran from the front of the cockpit to feed air to the well-developed Flat 12, with lower ducts to feed the radiators.

The dramatic season, documented in the movie Rush, saw Ferrari take six wins (five to Lauda, one to Regazzoni) in the first nine races, before that horrendous day at the Nürburgring, and Lauda's fiery crash. Lauda missed two more races before his unbelievably heroic return but, as the now legendary tale played out, he withdrew from a torrential Japanese Grand Prix finale, losing the title by a single point to Brit James Hunt (McLaren). Ferrari, as it had done the year before, did take the Constructors' title.

The team took a refined T2 into 1977, but it turned out to be a very open season, with teams such as Wolf (Jody Scheckter) and Lotus (Mario Andretti) fielding competitive cars. In the end, though, Lauda (with Carlos Reutemann now in the second car) ground out his second Drivers' championship (and again Constructors' for Ferrari), with two races to go.

Although contracted further, this was Lauda's 'screw you' moment and, still unhappy at the lack of support from Ferrari management following the 1976 crash,

declined to race at the last two races and left to join Brabham for 1978. His place was taken by a young Canadian – Gilles Villeneuve.

1978 wasn't a good year for Ferrari. Having decided to continue with the Flat 12, rather than head down the turbo path, it was a tough season – with Michelin expanding its F1 entry to include Ferrari and the development pains that went with it – and the 312T3 bowing to the awesome Lotus 78/79.

However, some significant aerodynamic gains with the T4 saw Ferrari, and Michelin, back on top in 1979, with Villeneuve and Jody Scheckter ultimately fighting it out for the title – the South African's consistency getting him over the line.

But that was to be the end of the Ferrari 'Flat 12' glory days – 1980 was a shocker, as the team worked to develop its all-new turbo-engined car alongside its final 'T' car, the 312T5. It was a shame – the last normally-

> ## "...significant aerodynamic gains with the T4 saw Ferrari, and Michelin, back on top in 1979..."

aspirated Ferrari Flat 12 didn't score a podium, the championship dominated by the superb 'aero' cars from Williams, Brabham and Ligier.

It was time to go turbo – but three Drivers' championships and four Constructors' crowns bear testament to a golden era for Ferrari and its classic 312T series.

FORZA GILLES!

Probably the last black and white image taken in Formula 1 – this evocative shot from the David Phipps Collection (Sutton Images) captures everything that Formula 1 fans remember of both the Ferrari 312T and the incomparable Gilles Villeneuve – right foot flat, and plenty of opposite lock. They don't build either of them like that any more... As was often the case that year, Gilles retired from this race – the 1978 South African Grand Prix, at Kyalami.

1976-1977

TYRRELL P34

INNOVATION UNFULFILLED

PATRICK

ERTL

elf

CITY

AL
RS CHECKS

FIRST
NATIO
CH

elf

elf

TYRRELL P34

Each-way bet? Four front wheels meant Tyrrell could try this unique mix-and-match of wet/dry tyres on a damp track!

One of the most revolutionary F1 cars ever was unveiled in time for the fourth race of the 1976 season, and while that year was primarily all about Hunt versus Lauda, McLaren versus Ferrari, the two radical six-wheeler Tyrrells, driven by Jody Scheckter and Patrick Depailler, were a sensational addition to the contest – finishing 1-2 in the Swedish GP and third and fourth respectively in the overall championship.

The theory behind the four small (10-inch) front wheels was straightforward – a reduction in front-end drag created by normal (larger) front tyres, increased tyre 'patch' area on the road (i.e. grip), and increased front brake disc area, and thus braking efficiency. It was the increased front mechanical grip which turned out to be the big plus, making the car more than competitive on tracks with a high proportion of sweeping corners, while the 'drag' gain was a little superficial – countered by the

"The theory... a reduction in front-end drag..."

"Remarkably, these tyres suited the car and its balance better than the originals and Tyrrell P34s started winning historic F1 events."

"It's a 'what could have been' case."

remaining huge rear tyre profile – although nevertheless improving air flow over the front half of the car.

A downside was the obvious doubling up of front suspension/brake systems, with the associated weight gain.

The car was the work of Tyrrell's chief designer Derek Gardner and, ultimately, relied on the supply of special 10-inch tyres from F1 tyre supplier Goodyear. For 1976 it produced a moderately balanced car but when, in 1977, Goodyear developed softer, grippier tyres for its regular cars (as it battled against newcomers Michelin at Renault), development of the special 10-inch front tyres lagged behind. The result – a car which understeered badly.

The team tried everything to resolve that issue – even widening the front track to aid grip – but by season's end, the decided to abandon the design and revert to a normal four-wheeled car.

Ironically, 20 years later, when the car started to appear in historic F1 racing, it did so on tyres produced by regular historic tyre suppliers Avon, who also produced a 10-inch version specifically to suit. Remarkably, these tyres suited the car and its balance better than the originals and Tyrrell P34s started winning historic F1 events, beating cars several seasons younger and thus more developed.

It's a 'what could have been' case.

LAST OF THE LEFT-FIELD THINKERS

Derek Gardner's Tyrrell P34 was the last of the truly radical F1 cars to race consistently – i.e. not be banned!

Brabham's revolutionary 'fan' car (with its enormous rear air-sucking fan and flexible sidepod skirts) appeared in 1978, at the Swedish Grand Prix, and won. Despite team owner Bernie Ecclestone's protestations that the fan was "for cooling purposes" (sure thing), he saw the point that to continue would force every team to build something similar and withdrew it from further competition before it could officially be banned.

The Tyrrell wasn't the only six-wheeler ever built. March, Ferrari, and – especially – Williams all built prototypes with four rear wheels, for similar aero/grip reasons. The Williams FW08D, which was tested in mid-1982, looked like it might be a world-beater, but it never raced. The FIA, using the same logic as the Brabham fan car, ruled that all F1 cars must have just four wheels.

Unsurprisingly, Lotus genius Colin Chapman was among those whose off-beat ideas got banned. In 1981, Chapman designed a 'twin chassis' car, the Lotus 88. It literally had two separate chassis – the driver in one (softly sprung), and the aerodynamic bodywork forming another. It was designed to get around the FIA ban on aerodynamic side 'skirts' touching the ground.

Drivers Elio de Angelis and Nigel Mansell reckoned it had potential, although detractors again pointed to excess weight. Some thought Chapman was going mad...

Regardless, as with the Brabham fan car, the rest of the teams reacted big-time, on the basis that the second chassis was "a moveable aerodynamic device", which was not allowed. The FIA agreed, and it all came to a head at the British Grand Prix when the FIA threatened to exclude the British GP from championship points allocation if the Brits allowed the Lotus 88B to race. They didn't and that, as far as the Lotus 88 went, was that. The Lotus 88/88B never raced.

It was also the last creation of design genius Chapman – he died just over a year later from a heart-attack. Or was it simply frustration at the constant stifling of his innovative ideas?

WILLIAMS 'SIX-WHEELER'

BRABHAM 'FAN' CAR

LOTUS 88 'TWIN CHASSIS'

1978-1979
LOTUS 79
'GROUND-EFFECTS' BECOMES THE BUZZWORD

LOTUS 79

"In its black JPS livery, the Lotus 79 (and 78) proved to be a beautiful, as well as successful, Formula 1 car, yet another ground-breaker from the House of Chapman."

The Lotus 79 was the first truly successful 'ground-effects' car, dominating Formula 1 in a rare manner for its era. It provided Mario Andretti with the 1978 Drivers' championship (Lotus took the Constructors'), he and team-mate Ronnie Peterson with four 1-2s, all from the 11 races contested after it was introduced at the sixth race of 1978 – the Belgian GP.

It was simple – if it finished, generally, it won.

It followed on from, and evolved ideas first pioneered a year earlier with the Lotus 78. There were so many new philosophies involved... where to start? While Chapman had mused over planes before, the de Havilland Mosquito fighter-bomber had caught his attention. Apart from the obvious concept of an inverted wing generating downforce for a car, he also noted the use of hot air outlets from wing-mounted radiators, designed to enhance lift for the plane. For the era, it was a relatively complex design and build process, involving chief engineer Tony Rudd and Peter Wright (both ex-BRM), and much rolling-road scale modelling in a wind tunnel.

The Lotus 78 was the first result of that work – an inverted 'wing' shape to the underside of the car; hot air outlets across the sidepods from radiators mounted at the front of long sidepods; sliding solid rubber side skirts to keep the air under the car and maximise the 'ground effect' (and actually hide the critical underside from prying opposition eyes!).

It was immediately and spectacularly successful, despite its centre of gravity being rather too far forward and thus needing a big rear wing to balance it, and Andretti won four races (along with one for team-mate Gunnar Nilsson). A rash of late-season retirements all that cost the 1977

championship (including the famous 'Tarzan' corner clash with a pushy James Hunt at the Dutch GP ...

The 78 remained in use for the first five races of 1978, Andretti and new team-mate Ronnie Peterson taking a win each, but then came the Lotus 79 – the car that took the 78 philosophies and refined them beautifully.

Extending the underfloor back beyond the front of the rear wheels provided the answer to the centre-of-gravity issue, allowing a smaller rear wing. Three fuel tanks (one behind the driver, one in each sidepod) now became one behind the driver. The reason for its late debut was spectacular – so good was the downforce that it placed doubts on the overall chassis strength. Strengthening around the tub area was required.

Andretti put the new car on pole on debut in Belgium, and he and Peterson completed the first of four 1-2 results – indeed for the rest of the season, Andretti either won or retired, and if he did retire, Peterson took over. Mid-season, Andretti contested eight races for five wins and three DNFs.

In its black JPS livery, the Lotus 79 (and 78) proved to be a beautiful, as well as successful, Formula 1 car, yet another ground-breaker from the House of Chapman. Perhaps his best.

But Formula 1 moves quickly and, for 1979, Ferrari, Williams and Ligier were among those 'cottoning on' to the ground effects principles and producing their own successful interpretations. What was expected to be Lotus' next step, the Lotus 80, simply didn't work (it was designed as a total front-to-rear wing car, but a porpoising effect made the downforce, while massive, rapidly variable – it was a monster to drive) and the season was dominated by those other teams as Lotus was forced to soldier on with an updated 79.

"While Chapman had mused over planes before, the de Havilland Mosquito fighter-bomber had caught his attention."

CRUEL FINALE

September 11, 1978, should have been a day of celebration for all at Lotus, but the day the 1978 F1 championship was won by Mario Andretti turned out to be one of several related tragic ones surrounding the team.

In practice, Ronnie Peterson had damaged his Lotus 79 beyond immediate repair and, as he couldn't fit into the team spare (built around Andretti) was forced to qualify in a back-up Lotus 78 – in a relatively lowly fifth.

The starter threw the green light too early – only the front few rows were stationary – and so a concertina effect grew as the midfield, including a slow-starting Peterson

headed towards Turn 1. A huge accident, involving 10 cars, saw Peterson sustain badly broken legs. It wasn't seen as life-threatening, but in hospital overnight his condition deteriorated due to 'fat embolism' and he passed away the following morning.

Back at the track, there had again been race start confusion as the race restarted three hours later, with the result that Andretti carried a one minute 'jumped start' penalty – turning a win into sixth place.

"...(the day) turned out to be one of several related tragic ones *surrounding the team.*"

It didn't matter – Peterson was the only remaining driver with a mathematical chance to deprive him of the championship, and the accident now ruled that out.

It was tough enough to deal with the fact that his team-mate had been badly injured, but then Mario and the team were shattered by the overnight tragedy.

There was ultimately more sadness to come. A month later, having been forced to quit F1 at the beginning of the year, Mario's 1977 team-mate Gunnar Nilsson lost his battle with testicular cancer. Then, some years later, in 1987, Petersen's shattered widow Barbro tragically committed suicide.

However, the Monza crash, and Petersen's unsatisfactory medical care on-track and in the immediate aftermath, would provide much of the motivation for Professor Sid Watkins' crusade for better medical back-up at F1 races. Appointed Safety and Medical Delegate by Bernie Ecclestone just weeks prior to Monza, he demanded both a medical car with doctor to follow the F1 field on its opening lap, and a medical helicopter, as a starting point for the massive progress he was ultimately able to make to Formula 1 safety and medical back-up.

1981-1983
McLAREN MP4/1
LIGHTER, FASTER, SAFER

McLAREN MP4/1

The McLaren MP4/1, and its handful of updates, was not ultimately a championship winner, but it paved the way for modern grand prix car design – it was the first to be constructed with a carbon fibre composite monocoque chassis. It was thus another of the most significant cars in Formua 1 history.

It followed a year of great change at McLaren when, under pressure from sponsors Malboro, McLaren MD Teddy Mayer was pretty much forced to merge with a Formula 2 team called Project Four, also sponsored by Marlboro and run by an up-and-coming ex-mechanic by the name of Ron Dennis.

Dennis had designer John Barnard working for him, who had become familiar with carbon fibre manufacture and reckoned a carbon fibre-built tub would be a big step up from the existing aluminium/honeycomb construction being used at the time. The new, larger organization was able to fund such a project and, in partnership with US company Hercules Aerospace, they conceived and built the McLaren MP4.

Originally, the concept had its skeptics – there were those who thought that the first serious bang would see the chassis explode into a ball of carbon dust. They were wrong. The 1981 Italian Grand Prix dealt with that concern when John Watson had a huge crash at the high-speed Lesmo 2. It ripped the engine and gearbox from the car, but the tub remained intact, and Watson unhurt. Within weeks, all serious F1 teams were working on carbon fibre cars.

LEFT and (inset) RIGHT: The McLaren MP4/1 provided an F1 milestone – switching from aluminium honeycomb construction to carbon fibre – lighter, stronger, safer.

> *"...there were those who thought that the first serious bang would see the chassis explode into a ball of carbon dust. They were wrong."*

"...The very first MP4 built turned out to be massively over-stiff and over-engineered..."

Weeks before Monza, Watson drove the Ford DFV-powered car to victory at the British Grand Prix, at Silverstone. It was McLaren's first F1 win for nearly four years.

The very first MP4 built turned out to be massively over-stiff and over-engineered, such was Barnard's conservatism concerning the overall strength of the carbon fibre. The revised chassis was thus made using less 'plies' of the space-age product, producing a superbly strong, stiff and light result. Hercules at this stage hadn't evolved the technology to encompass the curved shapes possible in modern carbon fibre construction, so MP4/1 was made up of five major components, all with flat rather than curved faces.

Regardless, it set Formula 1 on a new path.

In the end, MP4/1s, in four different evolutions, were used for just over two years. Latterly, in late 1983, an MP4/1E became the test bed for incorporation of Dennis' next big coup – the TAG turbo engine, a co-development between Techniques d'Avant Garde and Porsche, specifically to suit designer Barnard's structural and aerodynamic needs.

That in turn led to the McLaren MP4/2, which dominated Formula 1 in 1984 – the wily Niki Lauda paired with young Frenchman Alain Prost. The pair often lapped the field, and the championship became an in-house contest. Prost always outqualified his more experienced team-mate, but Lauda's racecraft stood him in good stead. With six wins to Lauda's five, Prost needed to win the final race, with Lauda third or worse.

From a lowly grid 11 qualifying spot, Lauda drove through the field, snatching second place, and the championship (by half a point), late in the race when Nigel Mansell spun out of that vital spot...

In 2015, McLaren's F1 cars have reached the MP4/30 designation with the introduction of Honda's all-new hybrid F1 engine – but the original MP4 (for McLaren Project Four) car, the MP4/1, remains in many ways the most significant of them all.

1988
McLAREN MP4/4-HONDA
SHOW TIME

McLAREN MP4/4-HONDA

All the elements came together again in 1988 for McLaren, which won 15 out of 16 races, with 10 1-2s, as Ayrton Senna and Alain Prost dominated in the sensational Honda-powered McLaren MP4/4.

This season represented the successful culmination of another of Ron Dennis' negotiation frenzies.

Conscious of the performance of Honda's brilliant V6 turbo engine – and with the team's TAG turbos now at the end of their development potential – and looking to bolster his line-up with the clearly talented Senna (who had been at Lotus-Honda), Dennis got to Honda via Senna, who had evolved an close personal relationship with the Japanese company.

The result was Senna to McLaren; Honda engines still at Lotus (albeit in year-old spec), but Williams losing their Hondas to McLaren (leaving Williams to do a deal to run normally-aspirated Judd engines – Williams, and Nigel Mansell must have been fuming).

The result was a superteam – Prost and Senna, Honda engines, and... the remarkable McLaren MP4/4.

In order to help teams relying on non-turbo engines, the turbo-powered cars would deliver approximately 300bhp less than in 1987 thanks to the FIA's 'pop-off' valves, which had been introduced in 1987 to restrict turbo boost to 4.0 bar. For 1988 this was to be reduced to just 2.5 bar, along with a reduced fuel tank capacity of only 150 litres (compared to a maximum of 215 litres for the normally-aspirated engines).

"Senna and Prost were three seconds a lap faster in qualifying than the third car – the Lotus driven by Nelson Piquet, powered by a similar Honda engine."

But McLaren was confident that its package would dominate – indeed, after his first test laps in the car, conducted just a week before the opening race, Prost told Dennis the championship was theirs.

The MP4/4 was effectively an evolution of the previous year's MP4/3, which was the first McLaren not designed by John Barnard, who had left the company – to head up Ferrari's new UK-based design centre!

MP4/3 and thus MP4/4 were designed by American designer Steve Nichols, under the direction of ex-Brabham designer Gordon Murray – now Technical Director at McLaren.

Murray's last Brabham's had taken a 'lowline' design approach, although BMW's four-cylinder turbo engine wasn't ideal for the best aerodynamic result. The V6 Honda, however, was. So the MP4/3, an MP4/3-Honda testbed, and then the definitive MP4/4 itself followed the lowline approach.

The result was a brilliant car and, what's more it also looked beautiful in a way not seen since Colin Chapman's Lotus 79. Not sitting on its laurels, Honda had actually redesigned its V6 to better allow for the higher fuel economy needed for the last turbo-engine season, but it was the aerodynamics of the McLaren which sealed the deal.

At Imola for round two, for example, Senna and Prost were three seconds a lap faster in qualifying than the third car – the Lotus driven by Nelson Piquet, powered by a similar Honda engine. The pair set faster race laps than anyone else had qualified at, and lapped the field.

The only race not won by the McLarens in 1988 was the Italian GP, where Prost had a rare engine failure and Senna tripped over a lapped back-marker near race end and put himself out. It did, however, provide an appropriate and emotional win for Ferrari on home turf just four weeks after the death of Enzo Ferrari...

The 1988 championship was one Senna/Prost title not decided by a collision! Going into Japan, Senna had seven wins, Prost six. After a shocking start, Senna drove through the field, then closed on Prost as it started to drizzle, passing as they lapped De Cesaris, and going on to a triumphant win and first championship. Prost, of course, wasn't happy – he'd actually scored more points but, with the best 11 results counting, Senna had won by three points, with eight wins and three seconds...

McLaren's 15 wins in a season (from 16 races) would not be eclipsed until 2014, when Mercedes would take 16 (from 19 races). However, in percentage terms, the MP4/4 remains the winningest grand prix car ever.

"...in percentage terms, the MP4/4 remains
the winningest grand prix car ever."

1992-1993

WILLIAMS
FW14B/15C

ON EVEN KEEL

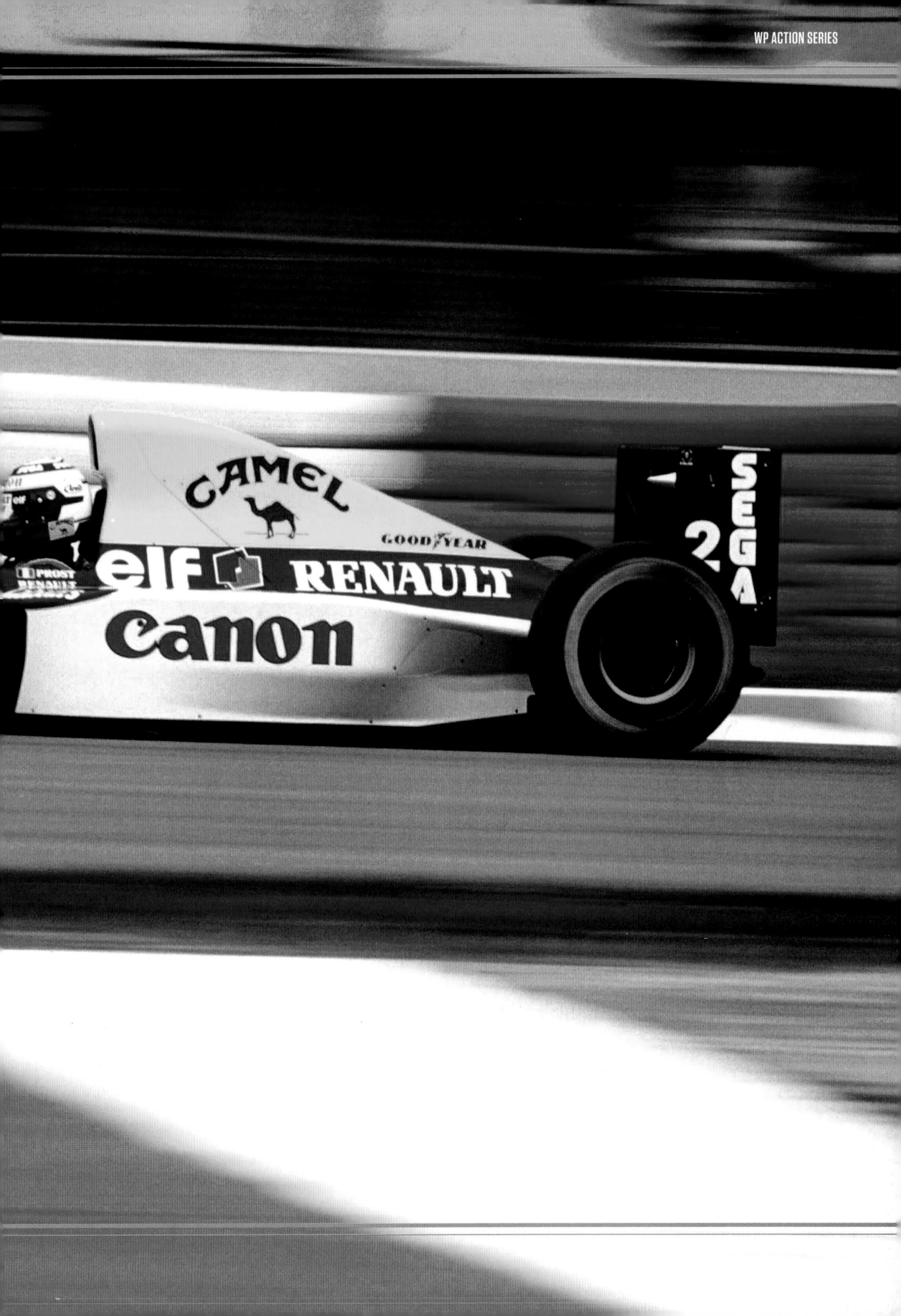
CAMEL
GOODYEAR
elf
RENAULT
Canon
SEGA
2
PROST

WILLIAMS FW14B/15C

> "By mid-season it was clear that the technology in the Williams FW15C was another case where every other serious team would need to go down the same path, at huge cost, to compete."

The Williams FW15 can best be described as the most sophisticated grand prix car ever built, an electronic masterpiece which was so successful that many of its 'driver aids' were ultimately banned.

The car was the first Williams car to be wholly designed around its amazing computer-controlled active suspension – and the first collaboration between resident technical chief Patrick Head and newly-signed designer Adrian Newey.

The previous (and successful) FW14B was originally a non-active (i.e. passive) suspension car which had been converted to the new technology – and delivered Nigel Mansell his world championship in 1992. Indeed, the purpose-built FW15 was ready to race from August 1992, but so dominant was the FW14B, with proven reliability, that Williams held back its ultimate masterpiece to 1993.

The team's only 'problem', as such, was its driver line-up. After a sabbatical year off (having been sacked by Ferrari), Frenchman Alain Prost had, using his Renault contacts, secured a two-year contract with Williams.

Mansell, defending world champion remember, had demanded clear number one driver status (and a fair pay rise) for 1993, which Williams was unwilling to agree to. Mansell thus walked out and went Indycar racing, leaving the team to promote test driver Damon Hill to the race team.

(Amid all this, Ayrton Senna, seeing the writing on the wall, had at one point offered to drive for Williams for nothing! Again, Prost's presence, and contract, specifically ruled out Senna, so that came to nothing. Indeed, a frustrated Senna would only drive his last year for McLaren – confined to 'customer' Ford engines after Honda's withdrawal – on a race-by-race basis. He did an amazing job, and was still in contention, mathematically, for the championship well into the season).

But there was little doubt that Prost and the Williams FW15C would take the title. Between seasons, the FIA had introduced narrower tyre widths and narrower track width in order to try and reduce speeds, so the original F15 had to be revised into a 15B. Then, with the driver situation sorted, came another problem – Hill was nearly

"...the most sophisticated grand prix car ever built, *an electronic masterpiece...*"

"The previous
(and successful)
FW14B... delivered
Nigel Mansell
his world
championship
in 1992."

30cm taller than Prost, and with feet to match. The solution was FW15C – built with two slightly different spec tubs, one of which accommodated Hill's large feet.

With Newey's aero-sensitive input, FW15C featured a narrower, raised nose, revised sidepods, and an all-up tidier packaging, along with a 760bhp Renault RS5 V10 engine. The list of technical features, refined from the FW14 included: computer-controlled active suspension, semi-automatic gearbox (which could be used as fully automatic on up-changes), and traction control, with ABS braking now added.

It was a space-age grand prix car for its time, the active suspension being the differentiating factor. Apart from the primary benefit of keeping the car as level as possible at all times, thus maximising the aerodynamic effects, there were additional smart tweaks – like a 'push-to-pass' button which simultaneously raised the rear of the car, reducing drag from the rear undercar 'diffuser' thus boosting straightline speed, while at the same time allowing the Renault to rev an additional 300rpm.

On the rare occasions when the Williams duo had to try and pass another car, it made it somewhat easier...

Downside? Only one – and any computer user will know that when a computer goes wrong, anything can happen!

So it was with the Williams FW15C – if the onboard computers misinterpreted the data they were receiving, things could get hairy. But this was a relatively rare occurrence the more time went by.

The team was dominant, only really challenged by the McLaren-Ford of Senna, who performed miracles with 70bhp less and no active suspension, winning three races in the first half of the season (including the brilliant wet Donington race) – but Prost won the remaining seven out of the first 10, and tied up the championship with four races still to go, during a period when team-mate Hill was starting to hit his straps, winning three in a row himself.

By mid-season it was clear that the technology in the Williams FW15C was another case where every other serious team would need to go down the same path, at huge cost, to compete. Amid criticism of too much electronic help and reduced driver input, all electronic drivers aids – active suspension, ABS, traction-control and launch-control – were banned, effective at the end of the season. The super hi-tech Formula 1 era was over.

So was the Prost era. The 'anti-Senna' clause in his contract tuned out to be for 1993 only. Faced with the imminent arrival of the Brazilian at Williams in 1994, Prost cut his career short and retired, as champion.

2002-2003

FERRARI F2002
THE PERFECT COMBINATION

FERRARI F2002

"Ferrari took the Constructors' championship with a points total more than all the other teams put together. That is domination."

The Ferrari/Schumacher era was an astonishing one for the Scuderia, reaping five consecutive Drivers' and Constructors' championships in five years, from 2000 to 2004 – a record that remains unmatched today.

Which of those remarkable five seasons produced the best of the Ferraris – like the defining Lotus 72, McLaren MP4/4 and Williams FW05C of earlier decades?

The F2002 was clearly the most complete, successful car, introduced three races into the 2002 season (Schumacher had a win and a third in the two season openers using the previous year's F2001). Of the remaining 15 races of 2002, the car won 14 – Schumacher took 10 of them, team-mate Rubens Barrichello the other four. Schumacher was second on all those four occasions – i.e. he won or was second in every race. The only race not won by the 2002 was Monaco, where for once (with an eye infection) Michael didn't qualify on the front row and found himself second, behind an impressive David Coulthard (McLaren), when crunch time came in the race.

The Drivers' championship was over with six, yes six, races to go... Ferrari took the Constructors'

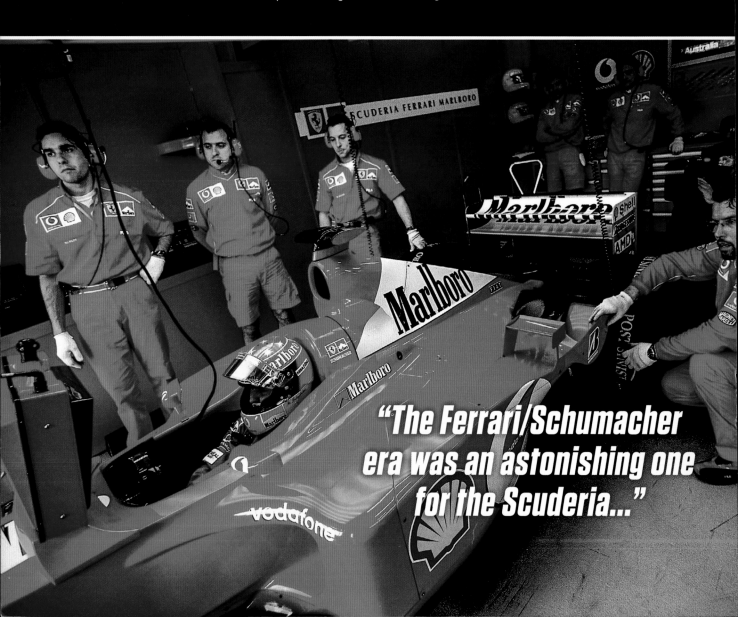

"The Ferrari/Schumacher era was an astonishing one for the Scuderia..."

"The F2002 was the almost perfect car for its time."

championship with a points total more than all the other teams put together. That is domination.

The ingredients for the 2002 were a refined version of the previous season's F2001, although a completely fresh design – a new Paolo Martinelli-designed 051 Ferrari 3-litre V10 low centre-of-gravity engine, lighter more tightly-packaged Rory Byrne chassis, with better-directed exhaust flow to assist the aero, and all-new titanium 'clutchless-change' gearbox. It was all matched, crucially, to tyres developed specifically for Ferrari by Bridgestone, making the most of improved weight distribution. And all under the watchful eye of technical director Ross Brawn.

In short, there wasn't a discernible deficiency anywhere in the team/car structure. The F2002 was the almost perfect car for its time.

2009
BRAWN BGP001
AN F1 FAIRYTALE

BRAWN BGP001

"They had to, effectively, cut 15cm (six inches) off the back of the tub to fit the Mercedes in. It was what could be described as a lash-up..."

The story of how the Brawn team and its Brawn BGP001 car came from nowhere to immediate grand prix success and the 2009 Drivers' (Jenson Button) and Constructors' championships is a modern fairytale. In a matter of weeks a team on the verge of closure was turned around and, literally throwing together a car with an engine it was never designed to use, went out and kicked butt. Amazing.

The story starts in 2007 and 2008, with a dispirited Honda F1 Racing Team pretty much propping up the

wrong end of the Formula 1 grid. The car simply wasn't good enough and drivers Jenson Button and Rubens Barrichello scored few points.

Former Ferrari technical guru Ross Brawn had been signed at the beginning of 2008 as team principal, too late to have any input into the 2008 car, so work actually began early on what was expected to be an all-new 2009 Honda-powered Honda F1 car.

Then came a bombshell. At the end of the season, in December, Honda's management announced it was pulling out of Formula 1. The global financial crisis was

Panasonic

"Its big performance plus was what was known as the 'double diffuser'..."

hitting hard and it couldn't justify the US$300m budget.

While the team continued work on the prototype car, a buyer would be sought to take over the team. Several interesting names came and went, but there was no buyer.

Brawn continued to tell his engineers and staff not to rush off to other employment; that the computer simulations for the new car were brilliant and that something would happen... and it did, at the very last minute. In fact, Brawn and CEO Nick Fry (who had been with the team since its pre-Honda British American Racing days) organised a management buyout when, in a partial change of heart, Honda agreed to provide a substantial part of the team running costs for one year. There was a month to go to the start of the season.

In the interim, Brawn had been looking at the engine options, and managed to put a 'customer' Mercedes engine deal together. Good in theory, but it created major technical problems – the crankshaft centre height was different from the Honda engine the car was designed for (affecting gearbox placement) and they had to, effectively, cut 15cm (six inches) off the back of the tub to fit the Mercedes in.

It was what could be described as a lash-up...

However, the design that had shown up so well in computer simulations still delivered. Its big performance plus was what was known as the 'double diffuser' – literally a double-layered rear underfloor which extracted under-car air very effectively. Brawn's design was superior thanks to a simple hole in the rear of the diffuser – someone had discovered that this further increased the speed of the air exiting via the diffuser, creating better downforce. Such are the

INDIA   BUTTON   BRAWN

The Brawn team arrived at the first race, in Melbourne, with little sponsorship on the cars, but with a technical tweak that would allow it to dominate.

minute aero gains and losses in modern F1. The 'hole' was protested by opposing teams, but declared legal.

Along with the rest of the generally much improved car, and despite the compromises which had been made, performance was immediately sensational.

The car ran for the first time in Spain, just three weeks before the season opener in Australia and was immediately faster than all the opposition who had been testing for weeks.

The story goes that a number of team mechanics and crew literally raced from the first day of testing to get to online bookies before they cottoned on and brought down huge championship odds offered for the unknown new team. At 200:1, several of them did quite well...

And so the team freshly renamed Brawn GP turned up to Melbourne, qualified 1-2 (Button-Barrichello), and

"Button then won five of the next six races."

ran 1-2 in the race. Button then won five of the next six races. Despite a mid-season drift, and without winning another race, Button accumulated enough points to lock away the Drivers' championship with a race to go.

It had been an amazing path from the depths of despair a year earlier, to world champions. Bizarrely, Mercedes engines powered the champions, with most of the budget coming from Honda. Pulling out was probably Honda's worst ever decision...

Mercedes itself had been contemplating entering F1 and at the end of the year bought Brawn and his partners out to create Mercedes F1. It had been one hell of a year.

2011
RED BULL RB7
NEWEY AT HIS BEST

RED BULL RB7

"Could it be said that F1 was starting to disappear up its own massively technical rectum at the cost of man-to-man racing – as some were now speculating?"

Among a four-season-long string of victories, and four Drivers' championship wins for young German Sebastian Vettel, the 2011 car, Red Bull's RB7 stands out as providing a particularly dominant performance.

The march of Red Bull Racing to the top of Formula 1 gained steam in 2006 when the well-funded team poached design guru Adrian Newey from McLaren, where he had masterminded championship wins in 1998 and 1999.

His first RB car, the RB3 was designed for 2007. It coincided with the team moving its Ferrari engine contract 'sideways' to its associate team, Toro Rosso, and switching to Renault engines designed with Newey's aero requirements in mind.

Sebastian Vettel joined Mark Webber at the team for 2009, finishing second in the championship (to the one-off 'miracle' Brawn) and so 2010 was seen as the team's first big championship chance.

The 2010 RB6 was a further evolution of the previous year's car and the season turned into a classic, with Vettel and Webber both in championship contention all the way, along with Fernando Alonso (Ferrari) and young star Lewis Hamilton (McLaren).

It was Webber's best title opportunity, but a spin out of the lead in the wet in Korea brought him back to the field, and it was Vettel who nailed his first title with wins in the final two races. The in-team tension between Vettel and Webber was year-long, intense and at times bitter, the latter (correctly) feeling that the team was favouring the German far too often. Roll on 2011.

The big change in Formula 1 for 2011 was the switch from long-term control tyre suppliers Bridgestone, to Pirelli, whose contribution to F1 would be softer tyre compounds designed to fade as part of putting on a show in the modern 'two tyre compound' races – something Bridgestone was a little loathe to do. Also introduced was DRS – the ability to open the rear wing flap and gain speed when within a second of the car in front at appointed track positions.

INSERT ABOVE:
Adrian Newey, here talking with Mark Webber, had already won world championships with Williams and McLaren before joining Red Bull and turning it into a championship steamroller. While tight regulations forbid radical innovation in modern F1, Newey must rank alongside the great Colin Chapman as a design 'great' of world motorsport.

There was a myriad of technical changes related to reducing the effect of rear diffusers, banning 'qualifying' engine mapping, along with a season-long debate over the legality of 'off-throttle blown diffusers', which saw engines stay at high revs under braking to create hot air flow and thus downforce. Yes, it had come to that... and hey, could it be said that F1 was starting to disappear up its own massively technical rectum at the cost of man-to-man racing – as some were now speculating?

In the event, Newey's 2011 RB7 joined the ranks of grand prix racing's most successful cars. It, and primarily Vettel, adapted best to the Pirelli switch and the other technical changes and racked up a season to remember: from 19 races RB7 started on pole 18 times (Vettel 15, Webber 3) and won 12 races (Vettel 11, Webber 1), and the Drivers' championship was all over with four races to go. The points gap in the Constructors', over McLaren Mercedes, was massive.

"...the four Constructors' titles won by Red Bull over this period brought to 10 the number won by Newey, at three different teams...""

As a matter of obvious relevance to a publication devoted to the best cars in Formula 1 history, the four Constructors' titles won by Red Bull over this period brought to 10 the number won by Newey, at three different teams – Williams 1992,93,94,96,97; McLaren 1998, Red Bull 2010, 11 12, 13. The four Drivers' titles, to Sebastian Vettel, add to the six (four at Williams, two at McLaren) Drivers' titles also overseen by Newey.

2014

MERCEDES W05
21ST CENTURY MASTERPIECE

MERCEDES W05

"...from the opening race of the season it was clear that the Mercedes W05 was the class act of 2014. It was the best, integrated, overall package, by some margin."

Pre-season testing involves much use of 'aero paint' (yellow) to show engineers just how air flows around the car.

Formula 1 history contains several examples of cars which, thanks to being well-designed and fully prepared for the introduction of a new formula – Ferrari's 1961 156 and Jack Brabham's 1966 Brabham-Repco are two classic examples – and the dominant Mercedes W05 Silver Arrow is another.

Having reduced the size of engines over the lead-up years to 2.4 litre normally-aspirated V8s (from 2006 to 2013), and overseen the introduction of Kinetic Energy Recovery Systems (KERS), which harvested 'kinetic' energy from braking systems into batteries which could then temporarily boost horsepower for passing, Formula 1 went the whole hog for 2014, with a massive change, carving the specs to 1.6 litre V6 turbocharged engines, but with Energy Recovery Systems (ERS) now an increased, integral and vital part of the package.

At the same time, fuel usage per race was slashed to 100kg (approx 140 litres), with a maximum 'flow rate' (ie consumption) of 100kg/hr. Obviously, this rate couldn't be maintained over a two-hour grand prix, but it also limited power available for qualifying. The engine rpm limit was also reduced, from 18,000rpm to 15,000rpm.

No longer would F1 simply have an engine. It would be a 'Power Unit', made up of an internal combustion engine (ICE) plus the energy recovery systems (ERS). To further technically challenge teams, cars were limited to just five Power Units for the whole season (down from eight previously) before grid penalties would apply.

KERS had now become ERS, the 'Kinetic' element of energy recovery, from braking, now added to by other recovery systems, including harvesting heat (and turning it too into electrical energy to power the electrical motor) from the turbocharger exhaust. A side effect of this, with

up to 90 percent of turbo exhaust output being 'harvested' was that not much actually exited via the traditional exhaust system – and the huge reduction in exhaust noise didn't hit the spot with many F1 fans brought up on the high-pitched whine of traditional engines.

The technical challenge was enormous, but one company – Mercedes-Benz – started its preparations well before any other and emerged with a clear winner.

Mercedes had become the nearest challenger in the last year of 2.4 litre F1 to the extraordinary dominance of the Red Bull-Renault team, winning three races in 2013, and thus evolving a quite competitive car, the WO4 in preparation for its long-planned 2014 challenger. The new 2014 regs were announced in mid-2011 and the company had

The ultimate 2015 Formula 1 Power Unit (the word engine is now not sufficient) – the Mercedes PU106A was radical and dominant.

"The key to the Mercedes W05's success was the PU106A hybrid Power Unit..."

already taken the decision to begin immediate, serious research, design, and development of its planned power unit from that day. Everything the Mercedes AMG Petronas did from that day was aimed at 2014.

The key to the Mercedes W05's success was the PU106A hybrid Power Unit (PU), allied to a carbon fibre-cased eight-speed gearbox. While the PU had an array of superbly integrated ERS inputs, its key innovation turned out to be the effective 'splitting' of the turbocharger, with the turbo (driven by hot exhaust gasses) and the compressor (feeding compressed, cool air to the engine) at different ends of the engine, joined by a shaft.

Mercedes had agreed to supply a number of customer teams – McLaren, Williams and Force India – none of whom had the advance design information to package the whole Power Unit into their cars in the exquisite way in which Mercedes did. Indeed, of the three it was Williams which made the best of it, regaining much of its former glory by season end, regularly 'next-best' to the rampant Mercedes team itself.

But from the opening race of the season it was clear that the Mercedes W05 was the class act of 2014. It was the best, integrated, overall package, by some margin.

Nearest non-Mercedes-powered car would be another Adrian Newey Red Bull, powered by a Renault hybrid PU

The 2014 championship soon became a two-man contest between Mercedes pair Lewis Hamilton and Nico Rosberg (smoking the tyres under braking), and 2015 began in similar fashion.

comparatively well-down on overall power output. It, in the hands of exciting new face Daniel Ricciardo – who all but destroyed defending world champion team-mate Sebastian Vettel (who would leave for Ferrari at the end of the season) – Red Bull won three races, each when the Mercs were affected by a reliability or intra-team driver clash problem.

Those aside, the 2014 Drivers' championship was a two-man race and could easily have become a boring procession at the front. Mercedes, to its credit, let Lewis Hamilton and Nico Rosberg slug it out, but in the end Hamilton prevailed, with 11 wins to five.

AND NOW?

Formula 1 has arrived at the end of its 65th year. The basic parameters for success remain the same as they did in 1950 in terms of the competition between car manufacturers and teams – innovation and preparation. But wow, has the technology level – as it has in day-to-day life – moved on in quantum leaps!

Where to now? Unless it is regulated, or banned, technology never moves backwards, nor race teams' desire to exploit it. The discussion remains one of athletic driver contest versus technological warfare.

There is a view that, as with the Williams FW15C, the ultimate high-tech car of its era, Formula 1 has again drifted too far from having sufficient driver input – although Mercedes' 2014 domination was no different to that of Lotus in the mid-60s and 1978 or McLaren in 1988. In the case of the Williams, the technology was banned; in the case of the others, the opposition simply caught up.

The international governing body of motorsport, the FIA, believes heavily in the promotion of 'green' ideals as the future for motorsport (hence its introduction of an electric engine-powered open-wheeler series in 2014, as well as pushing for the all-new hybrid F1 Power Unit). But is that what motorsport fans really want? Do they care? Do they yearn for the simpler, louder, dramatic days of the screaming V10s?

There are no simple answers. Life was simpler before mobile phones, Facebook and Twitter too, but in those cases there is no going back.

There will and must be restraints, from a cost perspective, on Formula 1, but the innovation and creativity that has driven it for the first 65 years isn't going to stop. Formula 1 has always been the bastion of experimentation and development of the automobile and that is unlikely to change.

Who can possibly imagine where Formula 1 will be in the next 10 years, never mind the next 65.

– Chris Lambden, April 2015